create
your
own
calm

With a
CLEAR HEAD
and a
QUIET HEART,
anything is
POSSIBLE.

create your own calm

A JOURNAL for QUIETING ANXIETY

Meera Lee Patel

First published in Great Britain in 2020 by LOM ART, an imprint of

Michael O'Mara Books Limited
9 Lion Yard
Tremadoc Road
London SW4 7NQ

Copyright © 2020 by Meera Lee Patel
Author photo credit: Nicola Harger

Published by arrangement with TarcherPerigee, an imprint of Penguin Publishing Group,
a division of Penguin Random House LLC

A CIP catalogue record for this book is available from the British Library.

Papers used by Michael O'Mara Books Limited are natural, recyclable products made from
wood grown in sustainable forests. The manufacturing processes conform to
the environmental regulations of the country of origin.

ISBN: 978-1-912785-41-4 in paperback print format

1 2 3 4 5 6 7 8 9 10
Book design by Meera Lee Patel
Printed in Germany

www.mombooks.com

To you,
for creating your own calm

INTRODUCTION

Across the entire world, the majority of us are living with rapidly increasing anxiety. The way it looks and feels is different for each of us, but the strange hum of it persists – accompanying us during errands, injecting itself into our conversations, and making it impossible to maintain a clear mind.

Anxiety alters how your brain processes thoughts and feelings, and it changes how your body responds to its environment. Anxiety stems from facing the unknown – in a volatile political landscape, through social injustices, academic or professional pressures, and even global crises. It also grows from the uncomfortable realization that we ourselves often feel unseen in our personal relationships.

In many ways, the world we live in today is designed to make us feel inadequate. How often do you feel the same familiar trickle of anxiety roll through you when you wake up each day and begin reading the morning news? How quickly does your mind begin to race when you take a look at your student loans or think about going back to school or work the next day? You aren't alone in feeling this way.

Feeling anxious is not your fault, nor is it an indication that something is wrong with you. Anxiety is a symptom of the many broken systems that we struggle to live within. Inequality in our communities, workplaces, and governments is a steady source of stress, fear, and disconnection.

Little things make me anxious, like mispronouncing a word or meeting someone new for the first time. Then there are the deep-rooted fears, the ones I've carried for years, that spin anxiety into me when I least expect it: the fear of worthlessness (or never being enough) each time I compare myself to someone else; the fear of failure that immediately sets in when I dare to dream a little bit bigger. The fear of rejection conjures intense anxiety when I am vulnerable in my work and in my relationships.

It's hard for me to admit (even to myself) that I'm an anxious person. I want to be courageous, not afraid – but my anxiety often convinces me that I am not brave.

For many years, wanting to be like everyone else in my life (or on the Internet) only made me more anxious. I tried to be where other people were in their careers and in their personal lives. I wanted desperately to reach the same life milestones my peers did – and this made me more anxious, too.

My fear determined what action I took and how I approached any new situation or relationship. My insecurity deepened and my anxiety grew louder, preventing me from living the life I wanted for myself. It prevented me from being the person I was, and shaped me into someone who never comfortably felt like herself. Anxiety created barriers between me and those who cared for me. I wasn't able to accept help from those who loved me. My anxiety also had physical symptoms: restlessness, headaches, and a rapidly beating heart that stopped me from leaving the house. For many, it feels worse.

To an anxious person, the idea that you can change your life is often impossible to imagine.

It was only when I began paying attention to myself – to my journey and the voice inside my own head – that I started to quiet the waves of anxiety that accompanied me. What I learned was that my anxiety is rooted in fear, and that the more I refuse to acknowledge or confront my fear, the stronger my anxiety becomes. What I learned was that a lot of my anxiety comes from pushing myself, including my strengths and my dreams, away.

What I learned was that my anxiety stems from not liking, accepting, or celebrating who I am.

This book is a journal for quieting anxiety. It is also a journal for self-acceptance. It helps you discover the peace that exists only when you feel content with who you are. It encourages you to look inside yourself to identify the roots behind your deepest (and often, most subtle) fears. It helps you dismantle your anxiety by offering techniques that quell the pangs of worry that stem from each fear. I share the practical methods for managing anxiety that helped me transition from living in fear to living in calm curiosity.

Have patience with yourself as you move through these pages at your own pace. Please remember that managing anxiety is a continual process: there is no one way to achieve peace of mind. Different methods work for different situations or periods in your life. The biggest gift you can give yourself is the chance to try again.

There is a light that exists in all dark places, and I hope these pages help you find it. Hold courage in your heart. The way you feel right now is temporary, and like everything else in life, it too will change. There are innumerable paths through the anxiety you feel, and this journal contains many of them. Each one will offer comfort for an anxious heart, lessons to carry with you, and challenges for you to navigate. Use what works and discard the rest.

Remember that if one road isn't a good fit, there are always several more: peace will inevitably follow you when you go your own way.

Work on releasing anxiety in your body:

1. Notice the places where your body feels tense or hardened.

2. Breathe in through your nose, and out through your mouth.

3. Repeat this exercise until the tension subsides.

BEFORE THIS EXERCISE, MY ANXIETY FELT LIKE:

AFTER THIS EXERCISE, MY ANXIETY FEELS LIKE:

List or draw three things that always
make you laugh and feel at ease.

TO LOVE ONE SELF IS THE BEGIN NING OF A LIFELONG ROMANCE.

Oscar Wilde, _An Ideal Husband_

List three ways you are hard on yourself.

1.

2.

3.

How can you support yourself more?

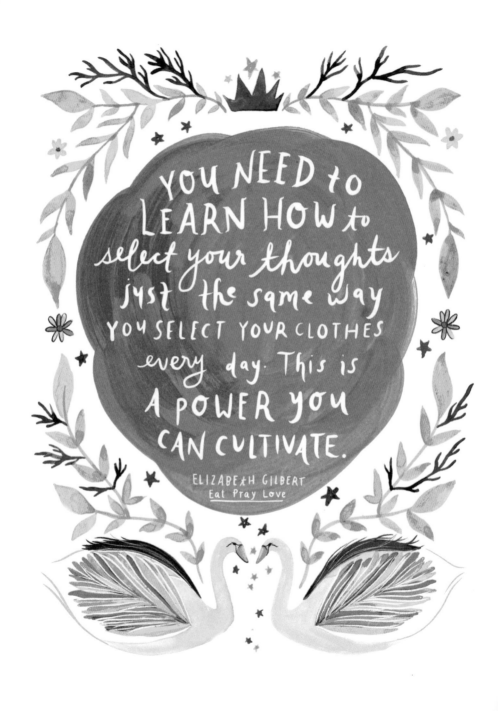

YOU NEED to
LEARN HOW to
select your thoughts
just the same way
YOU SELECT YOUR CLOTHES
every day. This is
A POWER YOU
CAN CULTIVATE.

ELIZABETH GILBERT
Eat Pray Love

Write down three anxious thoughts that frequently
enter your mind. What positive thoughts
can you replace each of these with?

1. Anxious thought:

   Positive thought:

2. Anxious thought:

   Positive thought:

3. Anxious thought:

   Positive thought:

The next time the anxious thought fills your mind,
choose to listen to the positive thought instead.

Understanding is the first step to acceptance, and only with acceptance can there be recovery.

J.K. ROWLING

HARRY POTTER AND THE GOBLET OF FIRE

Think about a difficulty you're currently experiencing.
What is the light in this situation?

you are never stronger...than when you land on the other side of despair.

ZADIE SMITH
White Teeth

What are you fearful about right now
that is making you anxious?

What is the likelihood this will actually happen?

What can you do if it does happen?

The source
of a true smile
is an awakened mind.

THICH NHAT HANH
Peace Is Every Step

What colour does your stress feel like?
Paint or colour it here.

What colour does your calmness feel like?
Paint or colour it here.

BE curious, NOT judg mental

Believing you can do something comes from a place of curiosity and confidence, while believing you should do something comes from a place of judgment. Learn to approach yourself with "can" instead of "should."

What is something you feel you should do?

Why do you feel you should do it?

Do you want to do it? (Circle one)

YES / NO

If the answer is no, what can you do instead?

I URGE YOU TO PLEASE notice, when you are happy, AND EXCLAIM OR MURMUR OR THINK AT SOME POINT, "If this isn't nice, I don't know what is."

KURT VONNEGUT
A Man Without a Country

List ten things you are grateful for.

1. _____

2. _____

3. _____

4. _____

5. _____

6. _____

7. _____

8. _____

9. _____

10. _____

We can easily forgive a child
who is afraid of the dark; the
real tragedy of life is when men
are afraid of the light.

PLATO

What values are most important to you?
Circle all that apply.

KINDNESS   GRATITUDE

                    STRENGTH   HUMILITY

             PERSEVERANCE   POSITIVITY

        PASSION   INTELLIGENCE   HUMOUR

             STABILITY   WEALTH

FREEDOM   INDEPENDENCE   MOBILITY

      HEALTH   WIT   CUNNING

             CAPABILITY   GENEROSITY

      ALTRUISM   ADMIRABILITY

             DEDICATION   WORK ETHIC

I had the epiphany that laughter was light, and light was laughter, and that this was the secret of the universe.

DONNA TARTT, THE GOLDFINCH

Close your eyes and imagine your most beautiful life.

What does it look like? Draw or describe it here.

True
happiness
is...
to enjoy the
PRESENT,
without anxious
DEPENDENCE UPON
the future.

LUCIUS ANNAEUS SENECA

What thoughts fill your mind when you feel anxious
about the future? List them here:

1.

2.

3.

Close your eyes and take five deep breaths.
What thoughts make you feel excited about the future?

1.

2.

3.

TO BELIEVE YOURSELF BRAVE IS TO BE BRAVE.

JOAN of ARC

What are five things you would do if
you didn't feel afraid?

1.

2.

3.

4.

5.

Now close your eyes and believe you are brave.
YOU ARE BRAVE.

How will you move toward each of these five things?

1.

2.

3.

4.

5.

THERE MUST BE LOTS OF MAGIC IN
THE WORLD ... BUT PEOPLE DON'T
KNOW WHAT IT IS LIKE OR HOW TO
MAKE IT. PERHAPS THE BEGINNING
IS JUST TO SAY NICE THINGS ARE
GOING TO HAPPEN UNTIL YOU MAKE
THEM HAPPEN.

Frances Hodgson Burnett
The Secret Garden

One of the best remedies for anxiety is being in nature.
Take a walk outside, being aware of everything around you.
Write down three things you see, feel, and hear.

1. I see:

2. I feel:

3. I hear:

WE OURSELVES FEEL THAT WHAT WE
ARE DOING IS JUST A DROP IN THE
OCEAN. BUT THE OCEAN WOULD BE
LESS BECAUSE OF THAT MISSING DROP.

Mother Teresa

List five things that ONLY YOU offer to the world.

1.

2.

3.

4.

5.

You
can't be
brave
unless you're
afraid.

A TIME I WAS AFRAID:

HOW I MOVED PAST MY FEAR:

When you arise
in the morning
think on what a
precious privilege
it is to live —
to breathe — to
think — to enjoy —
to love! MARCUS AURELIUS

Breathe in and out, focusing on the gratitude
you feel for a new day.

What is a thought you are grateful for?

What is a feeling you are grateful to experience?

What is something you feel grateful to have?

Who is someone you are grateful for?

IT ISN'T ENOUGH
TO TALK ABOUT
peace.

ONE MUST
believe IN IT.

AND IT ISN'T ENOUGH
TO BELIEVE IN IT.

ONE MUST
work AT IT.

ELEANOR
ROOSEVELT

Name the things that make you feel grounded and secure.

A PERSON:

A PLACE:

A BOOK:

A SONG:

AN ACTIVITY:

The strongest principle of growth lies in human choice.

GEORGE ELIOT
Daniel Deronda

Identify three habits you have that increase your anxiety. Circle the ones you can work on changing.

1.

2.

3.

Everything's a story.

YOU ARE A STORY.

I am a STORY.

FRANCES HODGSON BURNETT
A Little Princess

What story do you immediately tell yourself
when you begin to feel anxious?

What story can you tell yourself instead?

A JOURNEY OF A
thousand miles
BEGINS WITH
a single step.

LAO TZU

Think of something that makes you feel anxious.

Write about how you feel here:

Close your fists tightly and feel the tension.
Open and release them slowly. Repeat this ten times.

Write about how you feel now:

BEAUTY IS NOT
IN THE FACE; BEAUTY
is a light in the heart.

KHALIL GIBRAN

What are three things that give your life meaning?

Draw them here.

YOUR FEAR WILL ALWAYS LEAD YOU
to the magic.

My Friend Fear

What are two fears you'd like to work through?

FEAR #1:

Why I feel afraid:

What this fear is telling me I want most:

Instead of feeling afraid, I wish I felt:

I can begin feeling this way by:

FEAR #2:

Why I feel afraid:

What this fear is telling me I want most:

Instead of feeling afraid, I wish I felt:

I can begin feeling this way by:

YOU WILL BECOME WAY LESS CONCERNED WITH what other people think of you WHEN YOU REALIZE hOW SELDOM THEY DO.

DAVID FOSTER WALLACE
Infinite Jest

Our biggest anxieties can stem from feeling like an
outsider. When do you currently feel left out?

Around this person:

In this place:

When I am:

When I think about:

When I try to do this:

The secret of life, though, is
TO FALL
SEVEN TIMES
and to
GET UP
EIGHT TIMES.

PAULO COELHO
The Alchemist

Yesterday my anxiety felt like:

A DARK SHADOW

SHARP PAIN

DISCOMFORT

Today my anxiety feels like:

NEGATIVITY

PARALYSIS

DOUBT

Tomorrow, I hope my anxiety will feel:

LIGHTER

QUIETER

LESS OF
AN OBSTACLE

You are your best thing.

TONI MORRISON
Beloved

Imagine yourself in your ideal future.

1. Describe how you feel in this future:

2. What are the thoughts you have?

3. How do you spend your time?

4. What is the lesson you live by?

When one door
of happiness closes,
another opens;
BUT OFTEN WE LOOK
SO LONG AT THE
CLOSED DOOR THAT WE
DO NOT SEE
the one that has
been opened for us.

HELEN KELLER
We Bereaved

List something you've lost (a job, a relationship,
a loved one, a project) in the last year.

What are two positive things that came
from this experience?

1.

2.

NOTHING IN LIFE IS to BE FEARED, IT IS ONLY to BE UNDERSTOOD.

MARIE CURIE

What is a source of stress in each
of the following areas?

My health:

My creativity:

My family:

My friends:

At work/school:

On social media:

How can you eliminate some of these stressors?

For my health, I can:

For my creativity, I can:

With my family, I can:

With my friends, I can:

At work/school I can:

With social media, I can:

I once asked a bird,

"HOW IS IT THAT YOU FLY
IN THIS GRAVITY
of DARKNESS?"
She responded,

"LOVE LIFTS ME".

·HAFIZ·

What is the most recent thing someone else
did to lift your spirits?

What is the most recent thing you did
to lift someone else's spirits?

ONE
must still have
CHAOS
in oneself to be
ABLE TO GIVE BIRTH
-to a-
dANCING
STAR.

FRIEDRICH NIETZSCHE

Write down three things that make you feel nervous.

What is an exciting possibility that also exists
inside each of these?

1. What makes me nervous:

   A possibility that exists here:

2. What makes me nervous:

   A possibility that exists here:

3. What makes me nervous:

   A possibility that exists here:

everything has BEAUTY, but not everyone can see.

CONFUCIUS

List something beautiful about each of the following:

YESTERDAY:

TODAY:

A TIME YOU FELT ANXIOUS:

A TIME YOU FELT JOYFUL:

LAST YEAR:

NEXT YEAR:

A NEW OPPORTUNITY:

A MISTAKE:

A RAINY DAY:

"Dear old world,"
SHE MURMURED, "You are very
lovely and I am
glad to be alive in you."

L. M. MONTGOMERY
Anne of Green Gables

What sights and sounds make you feel most calm?

List or draw them here.

IF WE WAIT UNTIL WE'RE READY, WE'LL BE WAITING FOR THE REST OF OUR LIVES.

LEMONY SNICKET
The Ersatz Elevator

Think of a worry you wish you could leave behind.

Close your eyes and meditate on this worry for
five minutes, breathing in and out slowly and deeply.

When you open your eyes, let the worry go.

I exist
AS I AM,
THAT IS
enough.

-WALT WHITMAN-

Instead of telling yourself you should be somewhere else,
identify why where you are is enough.

FAMILY

I should feel:

Instead I feel:

What this is telling me:

WORK

I should be:

Instead I am:

What this is telling me:

SPIRIT

I should think:

Instead I think:

What this is telling me:

HEALTH

I should be:

Instead I am:

What this is telling me:

LOVE

I should feel:

Instead I feel:

What this is telling me:

All the variety, all the charm,
all the beauty of life is made
up of LIGHT and SHADOW.

LEO TOLSTOY
Anna Karenina

Choose three things you wish you could change
about your life. What is the light and dark of each one?

#1:

THE LIGHT:

THE DARK:

#2:

THE LIGHT:

THE DARK:

#3

THE LIGHT:

THE DARK:

Forever is composed of nows.

EMILY DICKINSON

List five things in your life that put you at ease.

1.

2.

3.

4.

5.

LIFE

CAN ONLY BE
UNDERSTOOD
BACKWARDS;
BUT IT MUST BE
LIVED
FORWARDS.

SØREN KIERKEGAARD

What are two lessons you've learned in the past year?
How have they affected the choices
you've made since?

Lesson #1:

Choices I made because of it:

Lesson #2:

Choices I made because of it:

The more one does
and sees and feels,
the more one is
able to do.

AMELIA EARHART

Write about a situation you encounter daily
that makes you nervous:

Close your eyes and visualize the situation going positively.
Imagine all the details and how peaceful you feel
throughout the experience.

How we
spend our days
is, of course,
how we spend
our lives.

ANNIE DILLARD
The Writing Life

LIST FIVE THINGS
YOU DO DAILY:

LIST FIVE THINGS
YOU WISH YOU DID DAILY:

1.

1.

2.

2.

3.

3.

4.

4.

5.

5.

So many things are possible just as long as you don't know they're impossible.

NORTON JUSTER
The Phantom Tollbooth

Write down three goals that feel impossible to you.

What is one step you can take toward
making each of them possible?

1. Impossible goal:

   Possible step:

2. Impossible goal:

   Possible step:

3. Impossible goal:

   Possible step:

I AM NO BIRD;
and NO NET ENSNARES ME;
I am a free human being
WITH AN INDEPENDENT WILL.

−CHARLOTTE BRONTË−

Jane Eyre

Write a letter to your past self, identifying the ways you've grown and moved through obstacles, fears, and anxieties. Include why you are proud of yourself for choosing to keep going.

Dear Self...

The willingness to accept responsibility for one's own life is the source from which self-respect springs.

JOAN DIDION
Slouching Towards Bethlehem

CIRCLE the ways you are already taking care of your
mind, body, and soul.

Then PLACE A STAR next to three things you will try
to include regularly.

SETTING BOUNDARIES   CALLING A FRIEND

            EATING HEALTHY FOODS   SLEEPING

        CARING FOR OTHERS   EXERCISING

            SOCIAL MEDIA DETOX

                    MEDITATING

EXPRESSING GRATITUDE

    SPENDING TIME WITH LOVED ONES

DANCING   LISTENING TO MYSELF   THERAPY

        TAKING TIME FOR MYSELF

SOMETHING
IN N ME
W E
KNOWS S WHERE
I AM GOING.

JACKSON POLLOCK

The Unknown can be a source of great anxiety and fear.
In these moments, it can be helpful to focus
on the things you feel confident of.

I KNOW:

I AM:

I FEEL:

I CAN:

I WANT:

IF I NEED HELP, I WILL ASK:

It will
never rain
roses: when
we want
to have
roses, we
must plant
more roses.

GEORGE ELIOT

What are four things you want to have more of?
How can you cultivate each in your life?

1)

2)

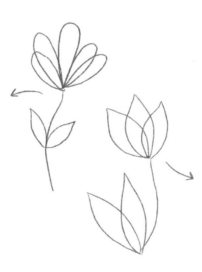

3)

4)

We are all strangers in a
strange land, longing for
HOME, but not quite
knowing WHAt or WHERE
home is.

MADELEINE L'ENGLE
The Rock That is Higher

When do you feel most peaceful?
Write or draw about it in this home.

nothing
I accept about
myself can be
used against me
to diminish
me.

audre Lorde
Sister Outsider

What is a trait (physical or emotional) you wish you could change about yourself?

List three ways this can be a source of strength for you.

1.

2.

3.

Within you,
there is a
stillness
AND A
sanctuary
to which you can
retreat at anytime
AND
be yourself.

HERMANN HESSE
Siddhartha

Step outside and breathe in air, sun, and trees.

Observe what you see, smell, and hear.

Notice how your mind quiets and your body relaxes.

Remember that there is always a new day close by.

THE MOST COMMON WAY PEOPLE GIVE UP their POWER IS BY THINKING they don't HAVE ANY.

Alice Walker

Describe (or think about) a situation
you currently feel powerless in.

What is one action you can take to change the situation?

WORST POSSIBLE OUTCOME:

BEST POSSIBLE OUTCOME:

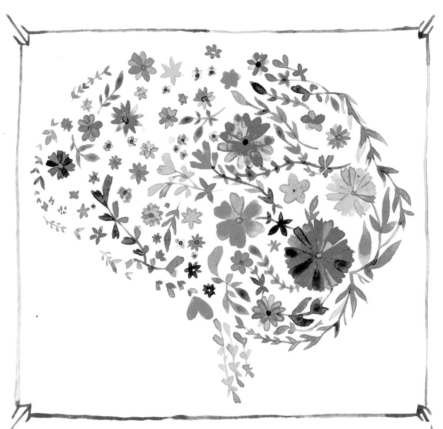

What you're supposed to do when you don't like a thing is CHANGE IT. If you can't change it, CHANGE THE WAY YOU THINK ABOUT IT.

MAYA ANGELOU

Wouldn't Take Nothing for My Journey Now

WHAT I DON'T LIKE   HOW I CAN CHANGE IT   HOW I CAN THINK
                                                         ABOUT IT

Life is like RIDING A BICYCLE

TO KEEP YOUR BALANCE, YOU MUST KEEP *moving.*

ALBERT EINSTEIN

ACTION CHANGES ATTITUDE.

What is one action that always resets your mood?

My advice is,

NEVER DO TOMORROW WHAT YOU CAN DO TODAY.

Procrastination is the thief of time.

CHARLES DICKENS
David Copperfield

I am avoiding _____

_____ .

because I'm afraid of

_____

_____ .

Reframe the task as a mantra that helps you
move forward with courage:

_____ is an opportunity for me

to grow, learn, and _____

_____ .

Repeat this mantra to yourself
as often as needed as you move forward.

IF you dare NOTHING, then when the day is over, NOTHING is all you will have gained.

NEIL GAIMAN
The Graveyard Book.

Write down three big dreams you are afraid of pursuing. Which fear is keeping you from pursuing each one? What action will move you past this fear?

1. BIG DREAM:

   Fear stopping me:

   Action that will move me forward:

2. BIG DREAM:

   Fear stopping me:

   Action that will move me forward:

3. BIG DREAM:

   Fear stopping me:

   Action that will move me forward:

IF ONE SCHEME OF HAPPINESS FAILS,
human nature turns to another;
IF THE FIRST CALCULATION IS WRONG,
we make a second better;
WE FIND COMFORT SOMEWHERE.

JANE AUSTEN
Mansfield Park

I PLANNED FOR THIS:

BUT INSTEAD THIS HAPPENED:

AND I GOT THROUGH IT BY:

Nothing contributes so much to tranquilize the mind as a steady purpose.

MARY SHELLEY
Frankenstein

What does a hopeful and secure future look like to you?

What are three steps you can take toward
building that future?

1.

2.

3.

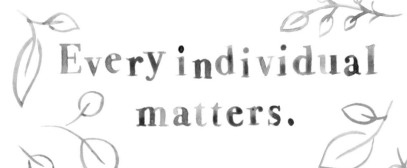

Every individual
matters.

Every individual
has a role to play.

Every individual
makes a difference.

JANE GOODALL

Fill out this Venn diagram about yourself.

WHY I MATTER

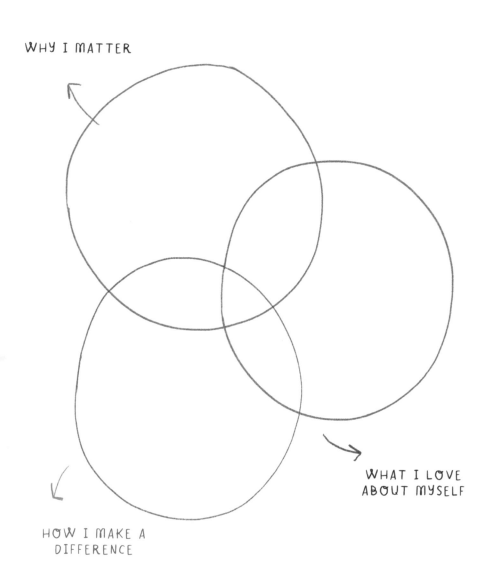

WHAT I LOVE
ABOUT MYSELF

HOW I MAKE A
DIFFERENCE

THERE ARE TWO WAYS of SPREADING
LIGHT: TO BE THE CANDLE or THE
MIRROR THAT RECEIVES IT.

EDITH WHARTON

Ways I can shine light and be supportive when...

A friend is disappointed:

I am disappointed:

A friend is feeling worried:

I am feeling worried:

A friend is scared:

I am scared:

A friend is excited:

I am excited:

A friend is sad:

I am sad:

ACKNOWLEDGMENTS

The exercises in this journal draw from my belief that there are countless ways to manage anxiety. I focus heavily on self-acceptance, because accepting who (and where) I am addressed my biggest source of anxiety: the battle between my heart, body, and mind.

In particular, the following practices greatly reduced the amount of anxiety I experience: daily meditation; regular exercise; creating meaningful connections (in my work, relationships, and with myself); spending ample time in nature; therapy; and finding self-worth outside of my career and accomplishments. Although I am not always successful, I try to keep my home and studio clean, because I find that a tidy space invites a tidier mind.

For further reading, I recommend *Lost Connections* by Johann Hari, which explores the disconnections that lead to sustained anxiety and depression.

I am grateful to all those who have crossed paths with me in recent years and contributed to my journey toward self-acceptance. You quelled so many of my fears along the way.

I have unwavering gratitude for my family and friends, who continually support me in moments of doubt and joy. I am very lucky to have you.

Many thanks to Laurie and Marian, who encourage me to use my voice. I am ever so grateful to you both.

BIBLIOGRAPHY

Quotations appear from the following publications:

Anna Karenina by Leo Tolstoy (Wordsworth Classics, 1997)

Anne of Green Gables by L. M. Montgomery (Signet, 2003)

The Alchemist by Paulo Coelho (HarperTorch, 2006)

The New Beacon Book of Quotations by Women by Rosalie Maggio (Beacon Press, 1992)

Beloved by Toni Morrison (Vintage, 2004)

The Best Liberal Quotes Ever: Why the Left is Right by William Martin (Sourcebooks, 2004)

Complete Works of George Eliot by George Eliot (Delphi Classics, 2012)

Conversations with Artists by Selden Rodman (Capricorn, 1961)

Daniel Deronda by George Eliot (Penguin Classics, 1996)

David Copperfield by Charles Dickens (Macmillan Collector's Library, 2016)

Einstein: His Life and Universe by Walter Isaacson (Simon & Schuster, 2007)

Eleanor Roosevelt, Voice of America broadcast (November 11, 1951)

The Ersatz Elevator by Lemony Snicket (HarperCollins, 2001)

The Fra: For Philistines and Roycrofters, edited by Elbert Hubbard, Felix Shay (Hubbard Journals, 1913)

Frankenstein: The 1818 Text by Mary Shelley (Penguin Classics, 2018)

The Gift: Poems by Hafiz, the Great Sufi Master by Hafiz (Penguin Books, 1999)

The Goldfinch by Donna Tartt (Back Bay Books, 2015)

The Graveyard Book by Neil Gaiman (HarperCollins, 2010)

Harry Potter and the Goblet of Fire by J. K. Rowling (Scholastic Paperbacks, 2002)

An Ideal Husband by Oscar Wilde (Project Gutenberg, 2009)

Infinite Jest by David Foster Wallace (Back Bay Books, 2006)

Jane Eyre by Charlotte Brontë (Bantam Classics, 1981)

The Journals of Søren Kierkegaard (Princeton University Press)

A Little Princess by Frances Hodgson Burnett (Puffin Books, 2014)

Mansfield Park by Jane Austen (Wordsworth Editions Ltd, 1998)

A Man Without a Country by Kurt Vonnegut (Random House Trade Paperbacks, 2007)

My Friend Fear by Meera Lee Patel (TarcherPerigee, 2018)

Our Precarious Habitat by Melvin A. Benarde (W. W. Norton & Company, 1973)

Peace Is Every Step: The Path of Mindfulness in Everyday Life by Thich Nhat Hanh (Bantam, 1992)

Personal Recollections of Joan of Arc, Volume 1 by Mark Twain (Project Guteberg, 2018)

The Annotated Phantom Tollbooth by Norton Juster (Knopf, 2011)

The Rock That Is Higher: Story as Truth by Madeleine L'Engle (Convergent, 2018)

The Secret Garden by Frances Hodgson Burnett (HarperClassics, 2010)

Siddhartha by Hermann Hesse (Samaira Book Publishers, 2018)

Sister Outsider: Essays and Speeches by Audre Lorde (Crossing Press, 2007)

Slouching Towards Bethlehem by Joan Didion (Farrar, Straus and Giroux, 2008)

Soaring Wings: A Biography of Amelia Earhart by George Palmer Putnam (1939)

Song of Myself by Walt Whitman (Dover Publications, 2000)

Stories Told by Mother Teresa by Edward Le Joly and Jaya Chaliha (Element Books, 2000)

Tao Te Ching by Lao Tzu (Harper Perennial Modern Classics, 2006)

Thus Spoke Zarathustra by Friedrich Nietzsche (Modern Library, 1995)

"Vesalius in Zante (1564)" by Edith Wharton in *North American Review* (November 1902)

We Bereaved by Helen Keller, (Leslie Fulenwider, 1929)

White Teeth by Zadie Smith (Vintage, 2001)

With Love by Jane Goodall (North-South Books, 1998)

The Writing Life by Annie Dillard (Harper Perennial, 2013)

Wouldn't Take Nothing for My Journey Now by Maya Angelou (Bantam, 1994)

ABOUT THE AUTHOR

MEERA LEE PATEL is a self-taught artist and writer who believes that anything is possible.

She is the author of *My Friend Fear: Finding Magic in the Unknown*, a beautiful meditation on fear and how it can help us become who we really are – if we let it.

She is also the author of the bestselling *Start Where You Are: A Journal for Self-Exploration* and *Made Out of Stars: A Journal for Self-Realization*.

She lives with her husband, dog, innumerable black vultures, wild turkeys, coyotes, and prancing deer on a farm in the northern woods of Nashville, Tennessee.

For more information, please visit meeralee.com or find her online @meeraleepatel.

ALSO BY

Meera Lee Patel

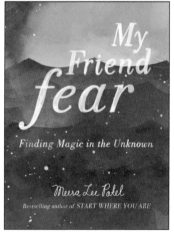

WWW.MEERALEE.COM